Summary

The United States faces the possibility of large economic losses from earthquake-damaged buildings and infrastructure. The Federal Emergency Management Agency has estimated that earthquakes cost the United States, on average, over $5 billion per year. California, Oregon, and Washington account for nearly $4.1 billion (77%) of the U.S. total estimated average annualized loss. California alone accounts for most of the estimated annualized earthquake losses for the nation.

A single large earthquake, however, can cause far more damage than the average annual estimate. The 1994 Northridge (CA) earthquake caused as much as $26 billion (in 2005 dollars) in damage and was one of the costliest natural disasters to strike the United States. One study of the damage caused by a hypothetical magnitude 7.8 earthquake along the San Andreas Fault in southern California projected as many as 1,800 fatalities and more than $200 billion in economic losses. An issue for the 112th Congress is whether existing federally supported programs aimed at reducing U.S. vulnerability to earthquakes are an adequate response to the earthquake hazard.

Under the National Earthquake Hazards Reduction Program (NEHRP), four federal agencies have responsibility for long-term earthquake risk reduction: the U.S. Geological Survey (USGS), the National Science Foundation (NSF), the Federal Emergency Management Agency (FEMA), and the National Institute of Standards and Technology (NIST). They variously assess U.S. earthquake hazards, deliver notifications of seismic events, develop measures to reduce earthquake hazards, and conduct research to help reduce overall U.S. vulnerability to earthquakes. Congressional oversight of the NEHRP program might revisit how well the four agencies coordinate their activities to address the earthquake hazard. Better coordination was a concern that led to changes to the program in legislation enacted in 2004 (P.L. 108-360).

P.L. 108-360 authorized appropriations for NEHRP through FY2009. Total funding enacted from reauthorization through FY2009 was $613.2 million, approximately 68% of the total amount of $902.4 million authorized by P.L. 108-360. Congress appropriated $131.2 million for NEHRP in FY2010, similar to FY2009 funding levels. Also, the American Recovery and Reinvestment Act (ARRA; P.L. 111-5) provided some additional funding for earthquake activities under NEHRP. What effect funding at the levels enacted through FY2010 under NEHRP has had on the U.S. capability to detect earthquakes and minimize losses after an earthquake occurs is difficult to assess. The effectiveness of the NEHRP program is a perennial issue for Congress: it is inherently difficult to capture precisely, in terms of dollars saved or fatalities prevented, the effectiveness of mitigation measures taken before an earthquake occurs. A major earthquake in a populated urban area within the United States would cause damage, and a question becomes how much damage would be prevented by mitigation strategies underpinned by the NEHRP program.

Legislation was introduced during the 111th Congress (H.R. 3820) that would have made changes to the program and would have authorized appropriations totaling $906 million over five years for NEHRP. Ninety percent of the funding would have been designated for the USGS and NSF, and the remainder for FEMA and NIST. The bill passed the House but not the Senate. Similar legislation will likely be introduced in the 112th Congress.

Contents

Figures

Tables

Contacts

Introduction

Close to 75 million people in 39 states face some risk from earthquakes. Earthquake hazards are greatest in the western United States, particularly in California, but also in Alaska, Washington, Oregon, and Hawaii. Earthquake hazards are also prominent in the Rocky Mountain region and the New Madrid Seismic Zone (a portion of the central United States), as well as in portions of the eastern seaboard, particularly South Carolina. Given the potentially huge costs associated with a large, damaging earthquake in the United States, an ongoing issue for Congress is whether the federally supported earthquake programs are appropriate for the earthquake risk.

Under the National Earthquake Hazards Reduction Program (NEHRP), the federal government supports efforts to assess and monitor earthquake hazards and risk in the United States. Four federal agencies responsible for long-term earthquake risk reduction coordinate their activities under NEHRP: the U.S. Geological Survey (USGS), the National Science Foundation (NSF), the Federal Emergency Management Agency (FEMA), and the National Institute of Standards and Technology (NIST). Congress last made changes to NEHRP in 2004 (P.L. 108-360), and authorized appropriations through FY2009 for a total of $902.4 million over five years. A bill introduced in the 111th Congress, H.R. 3820 (Title I), would have made further changes to the program and authorized appropriations through FY2014, but it was not enacted.

This report discusses:

- NEHRP—the multi-agency federal program to reduce the nation's risk from earthquakes;

- earthquake hazards and risk in the United States;

- federal programs that support earthquake monitoring;

- the U.S. capability to detect earthquakes and issue notifications and warnings; and

- federally supported research to improve the fundamental scientific understanding of earthquakes with a goal of reducing U.S. vulnerability.

National Earthquake Hazards Reduction Program (NEHRP)

In 1977 Congress passed the Earthquake Hazards Reduction Act (P.L. 95-124) establishing NEHRP as a long-term earthquake risk reduction program for the United States. The program initially focused on research, led by USGS and NSF, toward understanding and ultimately predicting earthquakes. Earthquake prediction has proved intractable thus far, and the NEHRP program shifted its focus to minimizing losses from earthquakes after they occur. FEMA was created in 1979 and President Carter designated it as the lead agency for NEHRP. In 1980, Congress passed the Earthquake Hazards Reduction Act (P.L. 96-472), defining FEMA as the lead agency and authorizing additional funding for earthquake hazard preparedness and mitigation for FEMA and the National Bureau of Standards (now NIST).

A Shift in Program Emphasis to Hazard Reduction

NEHRP's original focus on research to predict earthquakes was changed in 1990, when Congress enacted P.L. 101-614. Congress decreased the emphasis on earthquake prediction, clarified the role of FEMA, clarified and expanded the program objectives, and required federal agencies to adopt seismic safety standards for new and existing federal buildings. In 2004, Congress enacted P.L. 108-360 and adjusted the program again by shifting primary responsibility for planning and coordinating NEHRP from FEMA to NIST. P.L. 108-360 also established a new interagency coordinating committee and a new advisory committee, both focused on earthquake hazards reduction.

The current program activities are focused on four broad areas:

- developing effective measures to reduce earthquake hazards;

- promoting the adoption of earthquake hazard reduction activities by federal, state, and local governments, national building standards and model building code organizations, engineers, architects, building owners, and others who play a role in planning and constructing buildings, bridges, structures, and critical infrastructure or "lifelines";[1]

- improving the basic understanding of earthquakes and their effects on people and infrastructure, through interdisciplinary research involving engineering, natural sciences, and social, economic, and decision sciences; and

- developing and maintaining the Advanced National Seismic System (ANSS), the George E. Brown Jr. Network for Earthquake Engineering Simulation (NEES), and the Global Seismic Network (GSN).[2]

The House Science Committee report in the 108th Congress on H.R. 2608 (P.L. 108-360) noted that NEHRP has produced a wealth of useful information since 1977, but it also stated that the program's potential has been limited by the inability of the NEHRP agencies to coordinate their efforts.[3] The committee asserted that restructuring the program with NIST as the lead agency, directing funding towards appropriate priorities, and implementing it as a true interagency program would lead to improvement.

The 2004 law directed the Director of NIST to chair the Interagency Coordinating Committee. Other members of the committee include the directors of FEMA, USGS, NSF, the Office of Science and Technology Policy, and the Office of Management and Budget. The Interagency Coordinating Committee is charged with overseeing the planning, management, and coordination of the program. Primary responsibilities for the NEHRP agencies break down as follows (see also **Figure 1**):

---

[1] Lifelines are essential utility and transportation systems.

[2] ANSS is a nationwide network of seismographic stations operated by the USGS. GSN is a global network of stations coordinated by the Incorporated Research Institutions for Seismology (IRIS, a nonprofit organization). NEES is an NSF-funded project that consists of 15 experimental facilities and an IT infrastructure with a goal of mitigating earthquake damage by the use of improved materials, designs, construction techniques, and monitoring tools.

[3] U.S. House, Committee on Science, *National Earthquake Hazards Reduction Program Reauthorization Act of 2003*, H.Rept. 108-246 (Aug. 14, 2003), p. 13.

- NIST is the lead NEHRP agency and has primary responsibility for NEHRP planning and coordination. NIST supports the development of performance-based seismic engineering tools and works with FEMA and other groups to promote the commercial application of the tools through building codes, standards, and construction practices.

- FEMA assists other agencies and private-sector groups to prepare and disseminate building codes and practices for structures and "lifelines", and aids development of performance-based codes for buildings and other structures.

- USGS conducts research and other activities to characterize and assess earthquake risks, and (1) operates a forum, using the National Earthquake Information Center (NEIC), for the international exchange of earthquake information; (2) works with other NEHRP agencies to coordinate activities with earthquake reduction efforts in other countries; and (3) maintains seismic hazard maps in support of building codes for structures and lifelines, and other maps needed for performance-based design approaches.

- NSF supports research to improve safety and performance of buildings, structures, and lifelines using the large-scale experimental and computational facilities of NEES and other institutions engaged in research and implementation of NEHRP.

Figure 1. NEHRP Agency Responsibilities and End Users of NEHRP Outcomes

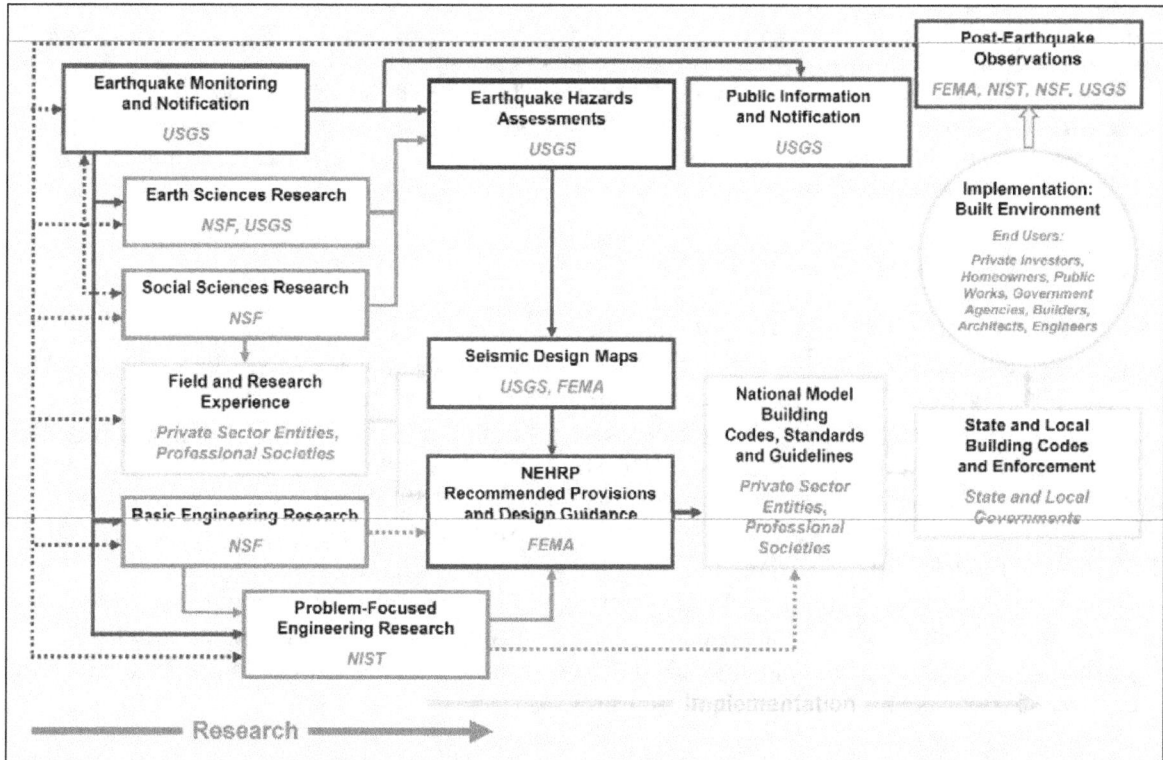

Source: NEHRP program office at http://www.nehrp.gov/pdf/ppt_sdr.pdf (modified by CRS).

Table 1 shows the authorized and enacted appropriations for NEHRP from FY2005 through FY2010. The total enacted amount for FY2005-FY2009 was $613.2 million, or 68% of the $902.4 million total amount authorized in P.L. 108-360 over the five-year span. President Obama requested a total of $129.7 million for NEHRP in FY2011, even though authorization of appropriations for the program under P.L. 108-360 expired at the end of FY2009.

Table 1. Authorized and Enacted Funding for NEHRP

($ millions)

		USGS	NSF	FEMA	NIST	Total
FY2005	Authorized	77.0	58.0	21.0	10.0	**166.0**
	Enacted	58.4	53.1	14.7	0.9	**127.1**
FY2006	Authorized	84.4	59.5	21.6	11.0	**176.5**
	Enacted	54.5	53.8	9.5	0.9	**118.7**
FY2007	Authorized	85.9	61.2	22.3	12.1	**181.5**
	Enacted	55.4	54.2	7.2	1.7	**118.5**
FY2008	Authorized	87.4	62.9	23.0	13.3	**186.6**
	Enacted	58.1	53.6	6.1	1.7	**119.5**
FY2009	Authorized	88.9	64.7	23.6	14.6	**191.8**
	Enacted	61.2	55.0	9.1	4.1	**129.4**
FY2010	Enacted	62.8	55.3	9.0	4.1	**131.2**
FY2011	Requested	62.3	54.3	9.0	4.1	**129.7**

Source: NEHRP program office, at http://www.nehrp.gov/pdf/2010NEHRPAnnualReport.pdf.

Notes: According to the NEHRP program office, ARRA funds are not included. The FY2011 requested budget is the estimated portion of the President's budget request that would be allocated for NEHRP activities. The FY2010 enacted amounts are estimates.

NEHRP Legislation in the 111th Congress

Title I of H.R. 3820, the Natural Hazards Risk Reduction Act of 2009, introduced in the 111th Congress, would have made changes to NEHRP and authorized appropriations for the program through FY2014. The bill was reported by the House Science and Technology Committee on February 26, 2010, and was passed by the House on March 2, 2010. The Senate did not act on the bill. The legislation would have retained NIST as the lead NEHRP agency, and authorized total appropriations of about $906 million over five years. Title II of H.R. 3820 would have made changes to the National Windstorm Impact Reduction Act (first enacted in 2004 as Title II of P.L. 108-360 and modeled after NEHRP), and Title III would have created an interagency coordinating committee, chaired by the Director of NIST, to oversee the planning and coordination of both the earthquake and wind hazards programs. The single interagency coordinating committee would have replaced the two separate interagency committees overseeing the current earthquake and wind hazards programs.

Earthquake Hazards and Risk

Portions of all 50 states and the District of Columbia are vulnerable to earthquake hazards, although risks vary greatly across the country and within individual states. Seismic hazards are greatest in the western United States, particularly in California, Washington, Oregon, and Alaska and Hawaii. Alaska is the most earthquake-prone state, experiencing a magnitude 7 earthquake almost every year and a magnitude 8 earthquake every 14 years on average. (See box below for a description of earthquake magnitude.) Because of its low population and infrastructure density, Alaska has a relatively low risk for large economic losses from an earthquake. In contrast, California has more citizens and infrastructure at risk than any other state because of the state's frequent seismic activity combined with its large population.

United States National Seismic Hazard Map

Figure 2 shows where earthquakes are likely to occur in the United States and how severe the earthquake magnitude and resulting ground shaking are likely to be. The map in **Figure 2** depicts the potential shaking hazard from future earthquakes. It is based on the frequency at which earthquakes occur in different areas and how far the strong shaking extends from the source of the earthquake. In **Figure 2**, the hazard levels indicate the potential ground motion—expressed as a percentage of the acceleration due to gravity (g). In a sense, the map shows the likelihood of where earthquakes could occur, and where the strongest shaking could take place.

Figure 2. Earthquake Hazard in the United States

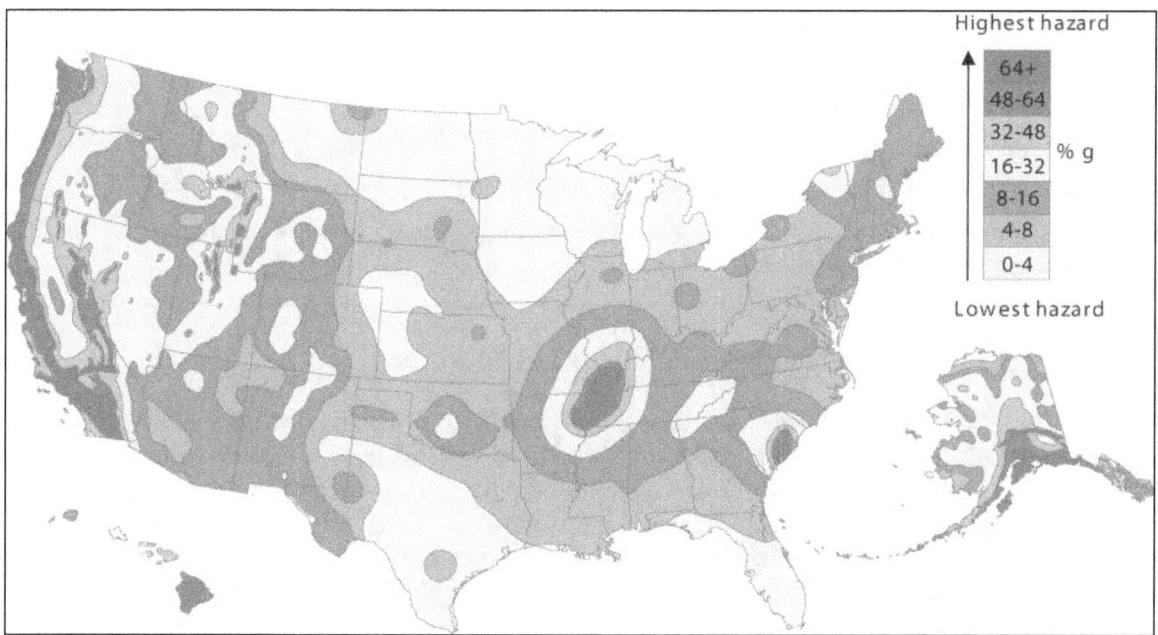

Source: USGS Fact Sheet 2008-3018 (April 2008), at http://pubs.usgs.gov/fs/2008/3018/pdf/FS08-3018_508.pdf. Modified by CRS.

Note: The bar in the upper right shows the potential ground motion—expressed as a percentage of the acceleration due to gravity (g)—with up to a 1 in 50 chance of being exceeded over a 50-year period.

Figure 2 also shows relatively high earthquake hazard in the Rocky Mountain region, portions of the eastern seaboard—particularly South Carolina—and a part of the central United States known as the New Madrid Seismic Zone (see "The New Madrid Seismic Zone" below). Other portions of the eastern and northeastern United States are also vulnerable to moderate seismic hazard. According to the USGS, 75 million people in 39 states are subject to "significant risk."[4]

Earthquake Magnitude and Intensity

Earthquake magnitude is a number that characterizes the relative size of an earthquake. It was historically reported using the *Richter* scale (magnitudes in this report are generally consistent with the Richter scale). Richter magnitude is calculated from the strongest seismic wave recorded from the earthquake, and is based on a logarithmic (base 10) scale: for each whole number increase in the Richter scale, the ground motion increases by 10 times. The amount of energy released per whole number increase, however, goes up by a factor of 32. The *moment magnitude* scale is another expression of earthquake size, or energy released during an earthquake, that roughly corresponds to the Richter magnitude and is used by most seismologists because it more accurately describes the size of very large earthquakes. Sometimes earthquakes will be reported using qualitative terms, such as Great or Moderate. Generally, these terms refer to magnitudes as follows: Great (M>8); Major (M>7); Strong (M>6); Moderate (M>5); Light (M>4); Minor (M>3); and Micro (M<3).

Intensity is a measure of how much shaking occurred at a site based on observations and amount of damage. Intensity is usually reported on the Modified Mercalli Intensity Scale as a Roman numeral ranging from I (not felt) to XII (total destruction). The intensity of an earthquake depends on where the earthquake occurs, how it is felt by people, and the damage it causes. The lower numbers of the Modified Mercalli Intensity Scale generally refer to how the earthquake is felt by people, and the higher numbers are based on observed structural damage.

Modified Mercalli intensities that are typically observed at locations near the epicenters of earthquakes of different magnitudes are as follows:

Magnitude 1.0-3.0   Modified Mercalli Intensity I

Magnitude 3.0-3.9   Modified Mercalli Intensity II-III

Magnitude 4.0-4.9   Modified Mercalli Intensity IV-V

Magnitude 5.0-5.9   Modified Mercalli Intensity VI-VII

Magnitude 6.0-6.9   Modified Mercalli Intensity VII-IX

Magnitude 7.0+   Modified Mercalli Intensity VIII or higher

Source: USGS FAQs, at http://earthquake.usgs.gov/learn/faq/; and Magnitude/Intensity Comparison, at http://earthquake.usgs.gov/learn/topics/mag_vs_int.php.

2008 Update to the National Seismic Hazard Map

On April 21, 2008, the USGS released National Seismic Hazards Maps that updated the version published in 2002.[5] Compared to the 2002 version, the new maps indicate lower ground motions (by 10% to 25%) for the central and eastern United States, based on modifications to the ground-motion models used for earthquakes. The new maps indicate that estimates of ground motion for the western United States are as much as 30% lower for certain types of ground motion, called long-period seismic waves, which affect taller, multi-story buildings. Ground motion that affects

---

[4] U.S. Geological Survey, Dept. of the Interior, *Earthquake Hazards—A National Threat*, Fact Sheet 2006-3016, March 2006, http://pubs.usgs.gov/fs/2006/3016/2006-3016.pdf. During the period 1975-1995, only four states did not experience detectable earthquakes: Florida, Iowa, North Dakota, and Wisconsin. See USGS Earthquake Hazards Program, *Earthquake Facts*, at http://earthquake.usgs.gov/learn/facts.php.

[5] USGS Fact Sheet 2008-3018, "2008 United States National Seismic Hazard Maps" (April 2008), at http://pubs.usgs.gov/fs/2008/3018/pdf/FS08-3018_508.pdf.

shorter buildings of a few stories, called short-period seismic waves, is roughly similar to the 2002 maps. The new maps show higher estimates for ground motion for western Oregon and Washington compared to the 2002 maps, due to new ground motion models for the offshore Cascadia subduction zone. In formulating the 2008 maps, the USGS gave more weight to the probability of a catastrophic magnitude 9 earthquake occurring along the Cascadia subduction zone. The Cascadia subduction zone fault ruptures, on average, every 500 years, and has the potential to generate destructive earthquakes and tsunamis along the coasts of Washington, Oregon, and northern California.

Earthquake Forecast for California

According to a report released on April 14, 2008, California has a 99% chance of experiencing a magnitude 6.7 or larger earthquake in the next 30 years.[6] The likelihood of an even larger earthquake, magnitude 7.5 or greater, is 46%, and such an earthquake would likely occur in the southern part of the state. The fault with the highest probability of generating at least one earthquake of magnitude 6.7 or greater over the next 30 years is the San Andreas in southern California (59% probability); for northern California it is the Hayward-Rodgers Creek fault (31%). The earthquake forecasts are not predictions (i.e., they do not give a specific date or time), but represent probabilities over a given time period. In addition, the probabilities have variability associated with them. The earthquake forecasts are known as the "Uniform California Earthquake Rupture Forecast (UCERF)" and are produced by a working group composed of the USGS, the California Geological Survey, and the Southern California Earthquake Center.

How Many Earthquakes Occur Each Year?

The USGS estimates that several million earthquakes occur worldwide each year, but the majority are of small magnitude or occur in remote areas, and are not detectable. More earthquakes are detected each year as more seismometers[7] are installed in the world, but the number of large earthquakes (magnitude greater than 6.0)[8] has remained relatively constant. Between 2000 and 2008 there were between 2,261 and 3,876 earthquakes per year in the United States, according to the National Earthquake Information Center (NEIC). (See **Figure 3**.)

As **Figure 3** shows, about 98% of earthquakes detected each year by the NEIC are smaller than magnitude 5.0 (light earthquakes); only 63 earthquakes exceeded magnitude 6.0 (strong earthquakes) for the 10-year period (about 0.2% of the total earthquakes detected), for an average of about six earthquakes per year of at least 6.0 magnitude. Larger earthquakes, although infrequent, cause the most damage and are responsible for most earthquake-related deaths. The great San Francisco earthquake of 1906 claimed an estimated 3,000 lives, as a result of both the earthquake and subsequent fires. Over the past 100 years, relatively few Americans have died as a result of earthquakes, compared to citizens in some other countries.[9] Since 1970, three strong

---

[6] USGS Fact Sheet 2008-3027, "Forecasting California's Earthquakes—What Can We Expect in the Next 30 Years?" (2008), at http://pubs.usgs.gov/fs/2008/3027/fs2008-3027.pdf.

[7] *Seismometers* are instruments that measure and record the size and force of seismic waves, essentially sound waves radiated from the earthquake as it ruptures. Seismometers generally consist of a mass attached to a fixed base. During an earthquake, the base moves and the mass does not, and the relative motion is commonly transformed into an electrical voltage that is recorded. A *seismograph* usually refers to the *seismometer* and the recording device, but the two terms are often used interchangeably.

[8] See USGS "Earthquakes Facts and Statistics" at http://neic.usgs.gov/neis/eqlists/eqstats html#table_2.

[9] Estimates of earthquake-related fatalities vary, and an exact tally of deaths and injuries is rare. For more information (continued...)

earthquakes (greater than magnitude 6) in the United States were responsible for 188 of the 212 total earthquake-related fatalities. (See **Table 2**.)

Figure 3. Histogram of the Number of U.S. Earthquakes from 2000 to 2009 by Magnitude (1.0 to 6.9)

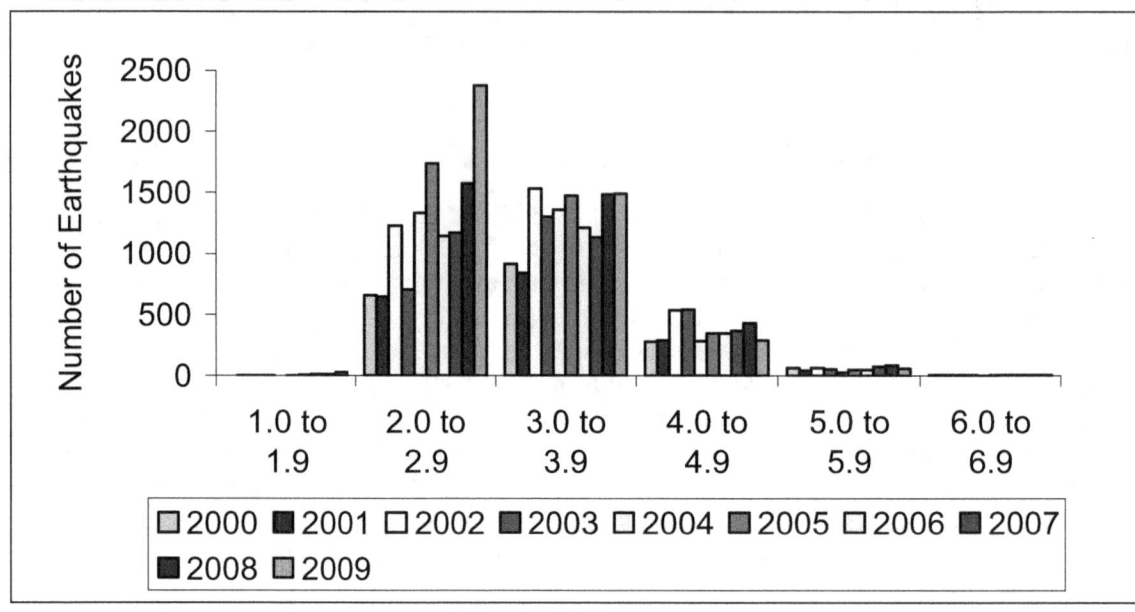

Source: USGS, "Earthquake Facts and Statistics," at http://neic.usgs.gov/neis/eqlists/eqstats.html; data as of January 6, 2011.

Note: Earthquakes greater than magnitude 7.0 and less than 1.0 are not shown. According to the USGS, 6 earthquakes of magnitude 7.0 or greater occurred in the United States between 2000 and 2009.

Table 2. Earthquakes Responsible for Most U.S. Fatalities Since 1970

Date	Location	Magnitude	Deaths
February 9, 1971	San Fernando Valley, CA	6.6	65
October 18, 1989	Loma Prieta, CA	6.9	63
January 17, 1994	Northridge, CA	6.7	60

Source: USGS, http://earthquake.usgs.gov/earthquakes/states/us_deaths.php.

Note: Other sources report different numbers of fatalities associated with the Northridge earthquake.

Earthquake Fatalities

Since 2000, only two deaths directly caused by earthquakes have occurred in the United States, both associated with falling debris in Paso Robles (CA) during the December 22, 2003, San Simeon earthquake of magnitude 6.5. In contrast, earthquakes have been directly or indirectly responsible for more than 685,000 fatalities in other countries since 2000.[10] Approximately 65%

(...continued)

on the difficulties of counting earthquake-related deaths and injuries, see http://earthquake.usgs.gov/regional/world/casualty_totals.php.

[10] U.S. Geological Survey, *Earthquakes with 1,000 or More Deaths Since 1900*, at http://earthquake.usgs.gov/earthquakes/world/world_deaths.php. This estimate does not include fatalities from the February 27, 2010, magnitude 8.8 Chilean earthquake, which has resulted in widespread destruction but few fatalities compared to the Indonesian, (continued...)

of those estimated deaths resulted from the December 2004 Indonesian earthquake (and resulting tsunami) of magnitude 9.1, and the January 2010 magnitude 7.0 earthquake in Haiti.

Estimating Potential Losses from Earthquakes

Estimating the seismic hazard for a region—as in **Figure 2**—is a first step in assessing risk. As a second step, shaking hazards maps are often combined with other data, such as the strength of existing buildings, to estimate possible damage in an area due to an earthquake. A third step in estimating potential losses would be in assigning value to the infrastructure at risk from earthquake damage. The combination of seismic risk, population, and vulnerable infrastructure can help improve the understanding of which urban areas across the United States face risks from earthquake hazards that may not be immediately obvious from the probability maps of shaking hazards alone, and what potential economic costs may be at stake.

The 1994 Northridge earthquake was the nation's most damaging earthquake in the past 100 years, preceded five years earlier by the second-most costly earthquake—Loma Prieta. Comparing losses between different earthquakes, and between earthquakes and other disasters such as hurricanes, can be difficult because of the different ways losses are calculated. Calculations may include a combination of insured losses, uninsured losses, and estimates of lost economic activity.

The United States faces potentially large total losses due to earthquake-caused damage to buildings and infrastructure and lost economic activity. As urban development continues in earthquake-prone regions in the United States, concerns are increasing about the exposure of the built environment, including utilities and transportation systems, to potential earthquake damage.[11] One estimate of economic loss from a severe earthquake in the Los Angeles area is over $500 billion.[12] Another estimate of economic loss from a hypothetical 6.5 magnitude earthquake along the heavily populated central New Jersey-Philadelphia corridor would be even higher—approximately $900 billion. The seismic hazard in the New Jersey-Philadelphia regions, however, is much lower than in the Los Angeles area, as shown in **Figure 2**.

Another approach to estimating potential losses is to "normalize" the damage estimates from past earthquakes by adjusting for inflation, increases in wealth, and changes in population. For example, adjusting the 1906 San Francisco earthquake and subsequent fire using 2005 dollars results in between $39 billion and $328 billion in losses, depending on assumptions and earthquake mitigation measures if that earthquake happened today.[13]

(...continued)

Pakistan, and Haiti earthquakes.

[11] FEMA Publication 366, *HAZUS MH Estimated Annualized Earthquake Losses for the United States* (April 2008), at http://www.fema.gov/library/viewRecord.do?id=3265. Hereafter referred to as FEMA 366.

[12] A. M. Best Company Inc., *2006 Annual Earthquake Study: $100 Billion of Insured Loss in 40 Seconds* (Oldwick, NJ: A.M. Best Company, 2006), p. 12. The A. M. Best report includes estimates from catastrophe-modeling companies of predicted damage from hypothetical earthquakes in Los Angeles, the Midwest, the Northeast, and Japan. The report cites an estimate by one such company, Risk Management Solutions (RMS), that a hypothetical 7.4 magnitude event along the Newport-Inglewood Fault near Los Angeles would cause $549 billion in total property damage. A hypothetical 6.5 magnitude earthquake along a fault between Philadelphia and New York City would produce $901 billion in total loss, according to an RMS estimate.

[13] Kevin Vranes and Roger Pielke, Jr., "Normalized Earthquake Damage and Fatalities in the United States: 1900-(continued...)

Some studies and techniques combine seismic risk with the value of the building inventory[14] and income losses (e.g., business interruption, wage, and rental income losses) in cities, counties, or regions across the country to provide estimations of economic losses from earthquakes. An April 2008 report from FEMA calculated that the average *annualized* loss from earthquakes nationwide is $5.3 billion, with California, Oregon, and Washington accounting for nearly $4.1 billion (77%) of the U.S. total estimated average annualized loss.[15] **Table 3** shows metropolitan areas with estimated average annualized U.S. earthquake losses over $10 million.

Table 3. U.S. Metropolitan Areas with Estimated Annualized Earthquake Losses of More Than $10 Million

(in $ millions)

Rank	Metro area	AEL	Rank	Metro area	AEL
1	Los Angeles-Long Beach-Santa Ana, CA	$1,312	23	Reno-Sparks, NV	$29
2	San Francisco-Oakland-Fremont, CA	$781	24	Charleston-North Charleston, SC	$22
3	Riverside-San Bernadino-Ontario, CA	$397	25	Columbia, SC	$22
4	San Jose-Sunnyvale-Santa Clara, CA	$277	26	Stockton, CA	$21
5	Seattle-Tacoma, WA	$244	27	Atlanta-Sandy Springs-Marietta, GA	$19
6	San Diego-Carlsbad-San Marcos, CA	$155	28	Bremerton-Silverdale, WA	$18
7	Portland-Vancouver-Carlsbad, OR	$137	29	Ogden-Clearfield, UT	$18
8	Oxnard-Thousand Oaks-Ventura, CA	$111	30	Salem, OR	$17
9	Santa Rosa-Petaluma, CA	$69	31	Eugene-Springfield, OR	$17
10	St. Louis, MO-IL	$59	32	Napa, CA	$16
11	Salt Lake City, UT	$52	33	San Luis Obispo-Paso Robles, CA	$16
12	Sacramento-Arden-Arcade-Roseville, CA	$52	34	Nashville-Davidson-Murfreesboro, TN	$15
13	Vallejo-Fairfield, CA	$40	35	Albuquerque, NM	$15
14	Memphis, TN	$38	36	Olympia, WA	$14
15	Santa Cruz-Watsonville, CA	$36	37	Modesto, CA	$13
16	Anchorage, AK	$35	38	Fresno, CA	$13
17	Santa Barbara-Santa Maria-Goleta, CA	$34	39	Evansville, IN-KY	$12
18	Las Vegas-Paradise, NV	$33	40	Birmingham-Hoover, AL	$11
19	Honolulu, HI	$32	41	El Centro, CA	$11
20	Bakersfield, CA	$30	42	Little Rock-North Little Rock, AR	$11
21	New York-Northern New Jersey-Long Island, NY	$30	43	Provo-Orem, UT	$10
22	Salinas, CA	$29			

Source FEMA Publication 366, *HAZUS MH Estimated Annualized Earthquake Losses for the United States* (April 2008). Annualized earthquake losses (AEL) calculated in 2005 dollars.

(...continued)

2005," *Natural Hazards Review*, vol. 10, no. 3 (August 2009), pp. 84-101.

[14] Building inventory refers to four main inventory groups: (1) general building stock, (2) essential and high potential loss facilities, (3) transportation systems, and (4) utility systems (FEMA 366).

[15] FEMA 366, p. 37.

Annualized earthquake loss (AEL) addresses two components of seismic risk: the probability of ground motion and the consequences of ground motion. It enables comparison between different regions with different seismic hazards and different building construction types and quality. For example, earthquake hazard is higher in the Los Angeles area than in Memphis, but the general building stock in Los Angeles is more resistant to the effects of earthquakes. The AEL annualizes the expected losses by averaging them by year.

A single large earthquake can cause far more damage than the average annual estimate. Annualized estimates, however, help provide comparisons of infrequent, high-impact events like damaging earthquakes with more frequently occurring hazards like floods, hurricanes, or other types of severe weather. The annualized earthquake loss values shown in **Table 3** represent future estimates, and are calculated by multiplying losses from potential future ground motions by their respective frequencies of occurrence, and then summing these values.[16]

Table 3 also shows that annualized earthquake losses in the New York-Northern New Jersey-Long Island metropolitan area are $30 million (ranked 21 out of 43 metropolitan areas with losses greater than $1 million per year), even though no destructive earthquakes have struck that area for generations.[17] This area has a relatively low seismic hazard, but also has an extensive infrastructure and is densely populated. That combination of seismic risk, extensive infrastructure, and dense population produces a significant risk to people and structures, according to some estimates.[18]

A Decrease in Estimated Loss?

In its most recent publication estimating potential earthquake losses, FEMA noted that the $5.3 billion in annualized earthquake loss nationwide was 21% higher than the $4.4 billion calculated in FEMA's previous report, published in February 2001.[19] However, the 2001 report calculated losses using 1994 dollars, and when adjusted to reflect 2005 dollars the earlier estimate increased to $5.6 billion, indicating a small decrease in nationwide annualized earthquake loss potential since the 2001 report was published. According to FEMA, this loss occurred even though the national building inventory increased by 50% over this same period.

What factors led to a decreased estimate in potential loss despite growth in building inventory? According to FEMA, two primary factors were responsible: (1) a slight decrease in estimated earthquake hazard in the western United States (namely California) except for some parts of Washington and Utah, and (2) a change in the distribution of building inventory in California, with an increase in wood frame buildings of 17% and a reduction in the amount of masonry (-6%), steel (-5.8%), and concrete (-3%) buildings in the state.[20] Wood frame buildings are less vulnerable to earthquake damage, generally, compared to other construction types. Because California accounts for 66% of the overall nationwide annualized earthquake loss, a 17% increase

---

[16] FEMA 366, p. 10.

[17] The largest earthquakes in New York, New Jersey, and Massachusetts were, respectively: 1944, Massena, NY, magnitude 5.8, felt from Canada south to Maryland; 1783, New Jersey, magnitude 5.3, felt from New Hampshire to Pennsylvania; and 1755, Cape Ann and Boston, MA, intensity of VIII on the Modified Mercalli Scale, felt from Nova Scotia to Chesapeake Bay (USGS Earthquake Hazards Program).

[18] USGS Circular 1188, Table 3.

[19] FEMA 366, p. 32.

[20] Ibid., p. 32 and p. 36.

in wood frame buildings had a proportionally large effect. In fact, FEMA attributed 78% of the loss reduction between 2001 and 2008 to the change in building inventory distribution, and 22% to the decrease in earthquake hazard for California.[21]

The New Madrid Seismic Zone

The New Madrid Seismic Zone in the central United States is vulnerable to large but infrequent earthquakes. A series of large (magnitude greater than 7.0) earthquakes struck the Mississippi Valley over the winter of 1811-1812, centered close to the town of New Madrid, MO. Some of the tremors were felt as far away as Charleston, SC, and Washington, DC. The mechanism for the earthquakes in the New Madrid zone is poorly understood,[22] and no earthquakes of comparable magnitude have occurred in the area since these events.

Estimating earthquake damage is not an exact science and depends on many factors. As described above, these are primarily the probability of ground motion occurring in a particular area (see **Figure 2**), and the consequences of that ground motion, which are largely a function of building construction type and quality, and of the level of ground motion and shaking during the actual event. Such factors contribute to the difficulty of making a reasonable damage estimate for a low-frequency, high-impact event in the New Madrid region based on the probability of an earthquake of similar magnitude occurring. This uncertainty has implications for policy decisions to ameliorate risk, such as setting building codes, and for designing and building structures to withstand a level of shaking commensurate with the risk. Presumably, the same seismic hazard should lead to similar building codes in urban areas (e.g., in **Figure 2**, compare the seismic hazard for the New Madrid area with portions of California).

Some researchers have questioned whether erring on the side of caution in the New Madrid Seismic Zone is justified.[23] These researchers challenge whether the benefits of building structures to conform with the earthquake probability estimates merit the costs, in light of the uncertainty in making those probability estimates.[24] These analyses may call into question whether the probability of ground motion estimates for the New Madrid Seismic Zone (the bulls-eye-shaped area shown in **Figure 2** that includes parts of Arkansas, Illinois, Tennessee, and Missouri), and other regions of the country that experience infrequent earthquakes, are too high.[25] A contributing factor to the uncertainty in estimating the earthquake hazard in the New Madrid Seismic Zone is the small amount of ground motion measured across the major faults, compared to much faster motions measured across major faults in California.[26] Typically, seismologists

---

[21] Ibid., p. 36.

[22] In contrast to California, where earthquakes occur on the active margin of the North American tectonic plate, the New Madrid seismic zone is not on a plate boundary but may be related to old faults in the interior of the plate, marking a zone of tectonic weakness.

[23] Andrew Newman et al., "Slow Deformation and Lower Seismic Hazard in the New Madrid Seismic Zone," *Science*, v. 284 (April 23, 1999), pp. 619-621.

[24] Seth Stein, Joseph Tomasello, and Andrew Newman, "Should Memphis Build for California's Earthquakes?" *Eos*, v. 84, no. 19, (May 13, 2003), pp. 177, 184-185.

[25] Seth Stein, "Code Red: Earthquake Imminent?" *Earth*, vol. 54, no. 1 (January 2009), pp. 52-59.

[26] Some researchers measure, for example, less than 2 millimeters of ground motion per year in the New Madrid Seismic Zone using modern GPS technology. In contrast, motion across the San Andreas Fault in California is about 36 millimeters per year. See Seth Stein, *Disaster Deferred: How New Science is Changing Our View of Earthquake Hazards in the Midwest* (New York: Columbia University Press, 2010), pp. 4-5.

---

estimate the stress that builds up on a fault by measuring ground motion across the fault: the faster the motion, the more quickly the stress builds up. The buildup of stress may be ultimately released in an earthquake during which the rocks on one side of the fault move relative to the other side. Generally, for fast-moving faults such as the San Andreas Fault, the period of earthquake recurrence is short compared to faults where the ground motion is relatively slow.

Yet despite the uncertainty raised by some researchers because of the apparent lack of much ground motion, the USGS attributes a seismic hazard to areas of the New Madrid Seismic Zone comparable to the most seismically active portions of California (see **Figure 2**), where earthquakes are much more frequent, and the mechanisms for generating earthquakes are better understood. The lack of much ground motion is a confusing factor for scientists trying to understand the New Madrid Seismic Zone, which experienced three major earthquakes 200 years ago but does not seem to exhibit much ground motion today. In part because of the 200th anniversary of the three major earthquakes, FEMA is planning a National Level Exercise (NLE 2011) that will focus on a scenario of a catastrophic earthquake in the New Madrid Seismic Zone and will encompass eight states: Alabama, Arkansas, Kentucky, Illinois, Indiana, Mississippi, Missouri, and Tennessee. The NLE 2011 will be conducted in May 2011.[27]

Earthquakes in Haiti, Chile, and Japan—Some Comparisons

The magnitude 8.8 earthquake that struck Chile on February 27, 2010, was over 60 times larger than the magnitude 7.0 earthquake that destroyed Port-au-Prince, Haiti, less than two months earlier. Yet the number of deaths and the amount of damage in Haiti far exceeded damage and fatalities in Chile. The Chile earthquake occurred offshore, and was deeper and farther away from major cities than the Haiti earthquake; in addition, the infrastructure in Chile—buildings, highways, bridges—appears to have been built to withstand earthquake shaking far better than similar infrastructure in Haiti. Japan's magnitude 9.0 earthquake on March 11, 2011, was even larger and more destructive than the Chile earthquake, but a large portion of the damage was caused by a powerful tsunami. The three countries faced significant seismic hazards, although the hazards facing Chile and Japan were arguably better known, because Chile experienced a great (magnitude 9.5) earthquake in 1960[28] and Japan experienced a very damaging earthquake in Kobe in 1995 and has a long history of seismic activity. By contrast, Haiti had last experienced a large earthquake in 1860 (earthquakes in 1751 and 1770 destroyed Port-au-Prince; the 1860 earthquake struck farther west). In addition to the seismic *hazard*, which is a consequence of geology and plate tectonics, Haiti's vulnerability to earthquake shaking appears to have exceeded Chile's. Japan's dense population and infrastructure, in particular the nuclear power reactors located on the northeast coastline close to the epicenter, increased its vulnerability to the March 11 earthquake and tsunami. However, Haiti was at greater *risk* of fatalities—from the earthquake and resulting damage to buildings—than Chile or Japan, even though Japan's March 11, 2011, earthquake was approximately 100 times larger than the Haiti earthquake.

---

[27] See FEMA, National Level Exercise NLE 2011 Private Sector Participation, at http://www.fema.gov/privatesector/take_action.shtm#2.

[28] According to the USGS, the May 22, 1960, magnitude 9.5 earthquake was the largest earthquake in the world. See http://earthquake.usgs.gov/earthquakes/world/events/1960_05_22.php.

January 12, 2010, Magnitude 7.0 Earthquake in Haiti

On Tuesday, January 12, 2010, a magnitude 7.0 earthquake struck Haiti at 4:53 p.m. The epicenter was located approximately 15 miles west-southwest of Port-au-Prince, and the earthquake occurred at a depth of about 8 miles, according to the USGS.[29] The relatively shallow earthquake, and its close proximity to the capital city, exposed millions of Haitians to severe to violent ground shaking. The earthquake occurred along the Enriquillo-Plantain Garden fault system, a major east-west trending strike-slip fault system that lies between the Caribbean tectonic plate and the North American tectonic plate; the Caribbean plate actively moves against the North American plate and shear stresses are created at the boundary. At a strike-slip fault, the rocks move past each other horizontally along the fault line (in contrast to a thrust fault, where rocks on one side of the fault move on top of the rocks on the other side). Other examples of strike-slip faults are the San Andreas fault in California and the Red River fault in China.

The January 12, 2010, earthquake caused widespread damage in the Port-au-Prince area, causing approximately 223,000 deaths and 300,000 injuries.[30] Also, a series of aftershocks followed the main earthquake. There were 14 aftershocks greater than magnitude 5, and 36 greater than magnitude 4, within the first day following the magnitude 7.0 event. Aftershocks have the potential to cause further damage, especially to structures weakened by the initial large earthquake. The USGS noted that buildings in the Port-au-Prince area will continue to be at risk from strong earthquake shaking, and that the fault responsible for the January 12, 2010, earthquake still stores sufficient strain to be released as a large, damaging earthquake during the lifetime of structures built during the reconstruction effort.[31]

The USGS based its probability estimates on techniques developed to assess earthquake hazards in the United States. Using these techniques, the USGS estimated that the probability of a magnitude 7 or greater earthquake occurring within the next 50 years along the Enriquillo fault near Port-au-Prince is between 5% and 15%. The range of probabilities reflects the current understanding of the seismicity and tectonics of the Haiti region. By comparison, the USGS has estimated that that the probability of a magnitude 7 or greater earthquake occurring within the next 50 years along the Hayward-Rodgers Creek fault east of San Francisco is about 15%.[32]

February 27, 2010, Magnitude 8.8 Earthquake in Chile

A magnitude 8.8 earthquake struck Chile on February 27, 2010, along a subduction zone plate boundary fault 65 miles north-northeast of the city of Concepcion and offshore of the Chilean coast.[33] The earthquake occurred at a depth of approximately 22 miles below the seafloor, much deeper than the earthquake that struck Haiti on January 12, 2010. The city of Concepcion experienced intensity IX shaking on the Modified Mercalli Intensity Index, corresponding to considerable damage to specially designed structures, and corresponding to great damage to "substantial" buildings. The capital city of Santiago, located 200 miles northeast of the epicenter,

---

[29] USGS Earthquake Hazards Program, at http://earthquake.usgs.gov/earthquakes/eqinthenews/2010/us2010rja6/.

[30] See http://earthquake.usgs.gov/earthquakes/eqinthenews/2010/us2010rja6/#summary.

[31] USGS statement, "USGS Updates Assessment of Earthquake Hazard and Safety in Haiti and the Caribbean," February 23, 2010, at http://www.usgs.gov/newsroom/article.asp?ID=2413&from=rss_home.

[32] Ibid. However, the USGS also notes that the probability of a magnitude 6.7 or greater earthquake occurring on the Hayward-Rodgers fault over the next 30 years is 31%.

[33] See http://earthquake.usgs.gov/earthquakes/eqinthenews/2010/us2010tfan/#details.

experienced intensity VIII shaking corresponding to considerable damage in ordinary substantial buildings.[34] The earthquake caused an estimated $30 billion in total economic damage.[35] Over 500 deaths were reported, many from the tsunami generated by the subsea earthquake, and approximately 1.8 million people were affected.

Because the earthquake occurred offshore, it generated a tsunami, which struck parts of the Chilean coastline and offshore islands, causing damage and fatalities. Tsunami warnings were issued by the National Weather Service Pacific Tsunami Warning Center for Hawaii, Japan, and other regions bordering the Pacific Ocean that may have been vulnerable to a damaging tsunami wave, although most regions far from the epicenter did not experience any serious damage. A tsunami caused significant damage to the city of Hilo, Hawaii, following the May 1960 magnitude 9.5 earthquake that also occurred along the subduction zone fault about 143 miles south of the February 27, 2010, earthquake.[36] Why the 1960 earthquake generated a tsunami that caused damage and fatalities in Hawaii, Japan, and the Philippines, while the 2010 earthquake did not, is not yet well understood and is being actively studied.

The magnitude 8.8 earthquake occurred along the boundary between the Nazca tectonic plate and the South American tectonic plate, which converge at a rate of about 3 inches per year. The Nazca plate is subducting under the South American plate, which rides over the top of the Nazca plate. In geologic terms, this is known as a thrust fault or megathrust, in contrast to a strike-slip fault, where the rocks on either side of the fault slide past each other. The San Andreas fault and the Enriquillo fault that caused the January 2010 Haiti earthquake are strike-slip faults. The Sumatran-Andaman megathrust fault, which triggered the December 2004 Indonesian earthquake and tsunami, is a subduction zone fault or megathrust geologically similar to the Nazca-South American tectonic plate subduction zone.

March 11, 2011, Magnitude 9.0 Earthquake in Japan

A 9.0 magnitude massive earthquake struck off Japan's northeast coast near Honshu on Friday, March 11, 2011 (12:46 a.m. eastern time in the United States). The earthquake triggered a tsunami that caused widespread devastation to parts of the coastal regions in Japan closest to the earthquake epicenter. The epicenter was located about 80 miles east of Sendai, and about 230 miles northeast of Tokyo, and it occurred at a depth of approximately 20 miles beneath the seafloor.[37]

The earthquake resulted from thrust faulting along the subduction zone plate boundary between the Pacific and North America plates, and this is similar tectonically to the motion described for the 2010 Chile earthquake. Where the earthquake occurred, the Pacific plate is moving westward and sliding underneath the North America plate at just over 3 inches per year. (See **Figure 4**.) This is similar to the convergence rate of the Nazca plate and the South American plate on the west side of Chile, where the February 27, 2010, earthquake occurred. The convergence zone between the Pacific plate and North America plate creates an undersea feature known as the Japan Trench. According to the USGS, tectonic plate motion in the Japan Trench subduction zone has

---

[34] See http://earthquake.usgs.gov/earthquakes/eqinthenews/2010/us2010tfan/#summary.

[35] Ibid.

[36] *The Orphan Tsunami of 1700—Japanese Clues to a Parent Earthquake in North America*, USGS, Professional Paper 1707, 2005, http://pubs.usgs.gov/pp/pp1707/.

[37] USGS, Earthquake Hazards Program, http://earthquake.usgs.gov/earthquakes/eqinthenews/2011/usc0001xgp/.

---

triggered nine magnitude 7 or greater earthquakes since 1973.[38] Also, records indicate that large offshore earthquakes occurred in the same subduction zone in 1611, 1896, and 1933, each producing tsunamis that caused great destruction and fatalities.[39] According to records, the 1896 earthquake created tsunami waves of over 100 feet high and a reported death toll of 27,000.[40]

Figure 4. Image of the Japan Trench and Location of the March 11, 2011, Earthquake

(the Pacific plate is moving west and underneath the North America plate)

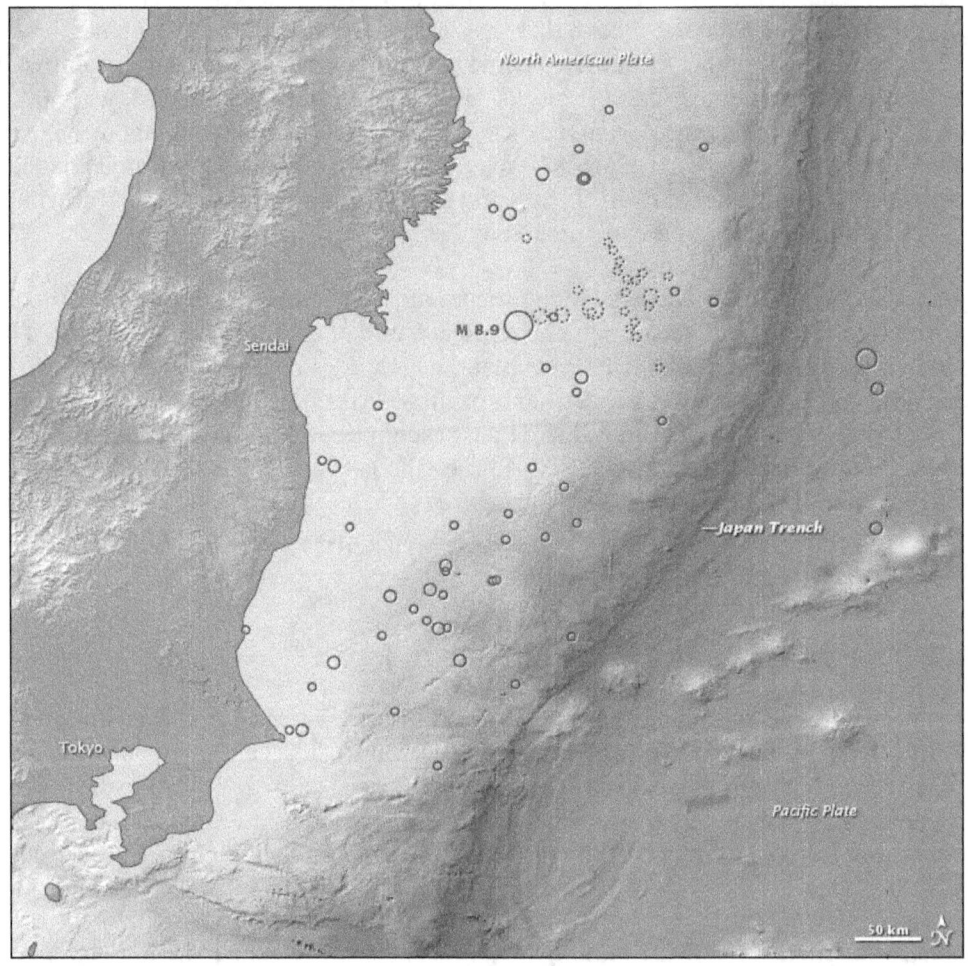

Source: NASA, Earth Observatory, March 11, 2011, http://earthobservatory.nasa.gov/NaturalHazards/view.php?id=49621.

Notes: Large circle depicts epicenter of the earthquake (upgraded to magnitude 9.0); solid circles indicate aftershocks, dotted circles indicate foreshocks (smaller earthquakes that occurred prior to the major earthquake).

---

[38] USGS Earthquake Hazards Program, http://earthquake.usgs.gov/earthquakes/eqinthenews/2011/usc0001xgp/#summary.

[39] Ibid.

[40] For more information on the March 11, 2011, Japan tsunami, and the U.S. tsunami monitoring network, see CRS Report R41686, *U.S. Tsunami Programs: A Brief Overview*, by Peter Folger.

Is There a Similar Risk to the United States?

Subduction zone megathrust faults generate the largest earthquakes in the world. The Cascadia Subduction Zone megathrust that stretches from mid-Vancouver Island in southern British Columbia southward to Cape Mendocino in northern California has the potential to generate a very large earthquake, similar in magnitude to the February 2010 Chilean earthquake and the March 11, 2011, Japan earthquake. The fault's proximity to the northwestern U.S. coastline—approximately 50-100 miles offshore—also poses a significant tsunami hazard; destructive waves from a large earthquake along the fault could reach the coast of Oregon and Washington in less than an hour, possibly in tens of minutes. The Cascadia Subduction Zone fault forms the boundary between the subducting Juan de Fuca tectonic plate and the overriding North America plate, very similar to the relationship between the Nazca plate and the South American plate off the Chilean coast, and the Pacific plate and North America plate east of Japan. If the Cascadia Subduction Zone megathrust were to "unzip" or rupture along a large section of its entire length, models indicate that it would likely generate a megathrust earthquake near magnitude 9 or more, similar to the 1964 Alaskan earthquake, the 1960 and 2010 Chilean earthquakes, the 2004 Indonesian earthquake, and the 2011 Japan earthquake. Scientists have documented that the last time this occurred along the Cascadia Subduction Zone fault was in 1700. The 1700 earthquake spawned a tsunami that traveled across the Pacific Ocean and struck Japan. Because of the similarities in the subduction zone megathrust faults, scientists hope to learn a great deal about the seismic hazard in the Pacific Northwest by studying the unique strong ground motion recordings from the 2010 Chilean magnitude 8.8 earthquake and the 2011 Japan earthquake.

Monitoring

Congress authorized the USGS to monitor seismic activity in the United States in the 1990 law modifying NEHRP (P.L. 101-614). The USGS operates a nationwide network of seismographic stations called the Advanced National Seismic System (ANSS), which includes the National Strong-Motion Project (NSMP). Globally, the USGS and the Incorporated Research Institutions for Seismology (IRIS) operate 140 seismic stations of the Global Seismic Network (GSN) in more than 80 countries.[41] The GSN provides worldwide coverage of earthquakes, including reporting and research.[42]

Advanced National Seismic System (ANSS)

According to the USGS, "the mission of ANSS is to provide accurate and timely data and information products for seismic events, including their effects on buildings and structures, employing modern monitoring methods and technologies."[43] If fully implemented, ANSS would encompass more than 7,000 earthquake sensor systems covering portions of the nation that are vulnerable to earthquake hazards. As envisioned, the system would consist of dense urban networks, regional networks, and backbone stations.

---

[41] IRIS is a university research consortium, primarily funded by NSF, that collects and distributes seismographic data.

[42] The GSN also monitors nuclear explosions.

[43] USGS Earthquake Hazards Program, http://earthquake.usgs.gov/research/monitoring/anss/.

ANSS Funding

Congress first authorized the ANSS program in P.L. 106-503 at a level of $38 million for FY2002 and $44 million for FY2003. The 2004 reauthorization of NEHRP (P.L. 108-360) authorized $30 million for ANSS in FY2005 and then $36 million per year through FY2009. From FY2000 through FY2010, the USGS has spent a total of $68.2 million on ANSS-directed funding,[44] although expenditures have never reached authorized levels since Congress first authorized appropriations for ANSS. Of the $8.8 million for ANSS-directed funding in FY2009, about $1.5 million was devoted to the development, modernization, and expansion of the system; the remainder of FY2009 funding was used to operate the existing system.[45] By the end of 2009, the USGS and its partners had installed a cumulative total of 886 ANSS earthquake monitoring stations.[46]

The American Recovery and Reinvestment Act (ARRA, P.L. 111-5) provided an additional $19 million for ANSS.[47] The ARRA funding for ANSS was provided for modernization of the current system, and is approximately 70% expended. The remainder of the ARRA funding for ANSS is expected to be expended by the end of FY2011.[48]

Dense Urban Networks

In the original conception for ANSS, approximately 6,000 of the planned stations would have been installed in 26 high-risk urban areas to monitor strong ground shaking and how buildings and other structures respond. Currently, five high-risk urban areas have instruments deployed in sufficient density to generate the data to produce near real-time maps,[49] called ShakeMaps, which can be used in emergency response during and after an earthquake.[50] (See "ShakeMap," below.)

Backbone Stations

Approximately 100 instruments comprise the existing "backbone" of ANSS, with a roughly uniform distribution across the United States, including Alaska and Hawaii. These instruments provide a broad and uniform minimum threshold of coverage across the country. The backbone network consists of USGS-deployed instruments and other instruments that serve both ANSS and the EarthScope project (described below, under "National Science Foundation").

---

[44] USGS FY2011 Budget Justification, p. J-9, at http://www.usgs.gov/budget/2011/greenbook/FY2011_USGS_Greenbook.pdf.

[45] Email from William Leith, Advanced National Seismic System Coordinator, USGS, December 22, 2009.

[46] USGS FY2011 Budget Justification, p. J-10.

[47] USGS FY2011 Budget Justification, p. J-10.

[48] E-mail from William Leith, USGS, January 11, 2011.

[49] The five urban areas are Los Angeles, San Francisco, Seattle, Salt Lake City, and Anchorage. E-mail from William Leith, USGS, February 7, 2011.

[50] The number of stations necessary to generate a data-based ShakeMap depends on the urban area and geology, but roughly correspond to about half the number of planned stations per urban area, at a spacing of about 20 kilometers between stations. Personal communication, William Leith, USGS, January 11, 2010.

National Strong-Motion Project (NSMP)

Under ANSS, the USGS operates the NSMP to record seismic data from damaging earthquakes in the United States on the ground and in buildings and other structures in densely urbanized areas. The program currently has approximately 1,280 strong-motion[51] instruments across the United States and in the Caribbean. The NSMP has three components: data acquisition, data management, and research. The near real-time measurements collected by the NSMP are used by other government agencies for emergency response and real-time warnings. If fully implemented, the ANSS program would deploy about 3,000 strong-motion instruments. Many of the current NSMP instruments are older designs and are being upgraded with modern seismometers.

Regional Networks

If ANSS were fully implemented under its original conception, approximately 1,000 new instruments would replace aging and obsolete stations in the networks that now monitor the nation's most seismically active regions. The current regional networks contain a mix of modern, digital, broadband, and high-resolution instruments that can provide real-time data; they are supplemented by older instruments that may require manual downloading of data. Universities in the region typically operate the regional networks and will likely continue to do so as ANSS is implemented.

Global Seismic Network (GSN)

The GSN is a system of broadband digital seismographs arrayed around the globe and designed to collect high-quality data that are readily accessible to users worldwide, typically via computer. Currently, 140 stations have been installed in 80 countries and the system is nearly complete, although in some regions the spacing and location of stations has not fully met the original goal of uniform spacing of approximately 2,000 kilometers. The system is currently providing data to the United States and other countries and institutions for earthquake reporting and research, as well as for monitoring nuclear explosions to assess compliance with the Comprehensive Test Ban Treaty.

The Incorporated Research Institutions for Seismology (IRIS) coordinates the GSN and manages and makes available the large amounts of data that are generated from the network. The actual network of seismographs is organized into two main components, each managed separately. The USGS operates two-thirds of the stations from its Albuquerque Seismological Laboratory, and the University of California-San Diego manages the other third via its Project IDA (International Deployment of Accelerometers). Other universities and affiliated agencies and institutions operate a small number of additional stations. IRIS, with funding from the NSF, supports all of the stations not funded through the USGS appropriations. Funding for the GSN is provided via annual appropriations from the USGS and the National Science Foundation. In addition, the USGS committed $4.7 million from ARRA funding to the GSN, and NSF committed a similar portion of its ARRA funding to replace obsolete equipment on GSN stations worldwide.[52]

---

[51] Strong motion seismometers, or accelerometers, are special sensors that measure the acceleration of the ground during large (>6.0 magnitude) earthquakes.

[52] USGS FY2011 Budget Justification, p. J-32. Annual appropriations for GSN totaled approximately $9 million for FY2009 and reflect the combined appropriations for USGS and NSF. The USGS portion of annual appropriations in (continued...)

Detection, Notification, and Warning

Unlike other natural hazards, such as hurricanes, where predicting the location and timing of landfall is becoming increasingly accurate, the scientific understanding of earthquakes does not yet allow for precise earthquake prediction. Instead, notification and warning typically involves communicating the location and magnitude of an earthquake as soon as possible after the event to emergency response providers and others who need the information.

Some probabilistic earthquake forecasts are now available that give, for example, a 24-hour probability of earthquake aftershocks for a particular region, such as California. These forecasts are not predictions, and are currently intended to increase public awareness of the seismic hazard, improve emergency response, and increase scientific understanding of the short-term hazard.[53] In the California example, a time-dependent map is created and updated every hour by a system that considers all earthquakes, large and small, detected by the California Integrated Seismic Network,[54] and calculates a probability that each earthquake will be followed by an aftershock[55] that can cause strong shaking. The probabilities are calculated from known behavior of aftershocks and the possible shaking pattern based on historical data.

When a destructive earthquake occurs in the United States or in other countries, the first reports of its location, or epicenter,[56] and magnitude originate either from the National Earthquake Information Center (NEIC), or from one of the regional seismic networks that are part of ANSS. Other organizations, such as universities, consortia, and individual seismologists may also contribute information about the earthquake after the event. Products such as ShakeMap (described below) are assembled as rapidly as possible to assist in emergency response and damage estimation following a destructive earthquake.

National Earthquake Information Center (NEIC)

The NEIC, part of the USGS, is located in Golden, CO. Originally established as part of the National Ocean Survey (U.S. Department of Commerce) in 1966, the NEIC was made part of the USGS in 1973. With data gathered from the networks described above and from other sources, the NEIC determines the location and size of all destructive earthquakes that occur worldwide and disseminates the information to the appropriate national or international agencies, government public information channels, news media, scientists and scientific groups, and the general public.

(...continued)

FY2010 was $5.8 million.

[53] USGS Open-File Report 2004-1390, and California 24-hour Aftershock Forecast Map, at http://pasadena.wr.usgs.gov/step/.

[54] The California Integrated Seismic Network is the California region of ANSS; see http://www.cisn.org/.

[55] Earthquakes typically occur in clusters, in which the earthquake with the largest magnitude is called the main shock, events before the main shock are called foreshocks, and those after are called aftershocks. See also http://pasadena.wr.usgs.gov/step/aftershocks html.

[56] The *epicenter* of an earthquake is the point on the earth's surface directly above the hypocenter. The *hypocenter* is the location beneath the earth's surface where the fault rupture begins.

With the advent of the USGS Earthquake Notification Service (ENS), notifications of earthquakes detected by the ANSS/NEIC are provided free to interested parties. Users of the service can specify the regions of interest, establish notification thresholds of earthquake magnitude, designate whether they wish to receive notification of aftershocks, and even set different magnitude thresholds for daytime or nighttime to trigger a notification.

The NEIC has long-standing agreements with key emergency response groups, federal, state, and local authorities, and other key organizations in earthquake-prone regions who receive automated alerts—typically location and magnitude of an earthquake—within a few minutes of an event in the United States. The NEIC sends these preliminary alerts by email and pager immediately after an earthquake's magnitude and epicenter are automatically determined by computer.[57] This initial determination is then checked by around-the-clock staff who confirm and update the magnitude and location data.[58] After the confirmation, a second set of notifications and confirmations are triggered to key recipients by email, pager, fax, and telephone.

For earthquakes outside the United States, the NEIC notifies the State Department Operations Center, and often sends alerts directly to staff at American embassies and consulates in the affected countries, to the International Red Cross, the U.N. Department of Humanitarian Affairs, and other recipients who have made arrangements to receive alerts.

ShakeMap

Traditionally, the information commonly available following a destructive earthquake has been epicenter and magnitude, as in the data provided by the NEIC described above. Those two parameters by themselves, however, do not always indicate the intensity of shaking and extent of damage following a major earthquake. Recently, the USGS developed a product called ShakeMap that provides a nearly real-time map of ground motion and shaking intensity following an earthquake in areas of the United States where the ShakeMap system is in place. **Figure 5** shows an example of a ShakeMap.

The maps produced portray the extent of damaging shaking and can be used by emergency response and for estimating loss following a major earthquake. Currently, ShakeMaps are available for northern California, southern California, the Pacific Northwest, Nevada, Utah, Hawaii, and Alaska.[59]

With improvements to the regional seismographic networks in the areas where ShakeMap is available, new real-time telemetry from the region, and advances in digital communication and computation, ShakeMaps are now triggered automatically and made available within minutes of the event via the web. In addition, better maps are now available because of recent improvements in understanding the relationship between the ground motions recorded during the earthquake and the intensity of resulting damage. If databases containing inventories of buildings and lifelines are available, they can be combined with shaking intensity data to produce maps of estimated damage. The ShakeMaps have limitations, especially during the first few minutes following an

---

[57] Stuart Simkin, NEIC, Golden, CO, telephone conversation, Nov. 4, 2006.

[58] In early 2006, the NEIC implemented an around-the-clock operation center and seismic event processing center in response to the Indonesian earthquake and resulting tsunami of December 2004. Funding to implement 24/7 operations was provided by P.L. 109-13.

[59] ShakeMaps for some areas outside the United States are also available. See http://earthquake.usgs.gov/eqcenter/shakemap/.

earthquake before additional data arrive from distributed sources. Because they are generated automatically, the initial maps are preliminary, and may not have been reviewed by experts when first made available. They are considered a work in progress, but are deemed to be very promising, especially as more modern seismic instruments are added to the regional networks under ANSS and computational and telecommunication abilities improve.

Figure 5. Example of a ShakeMap

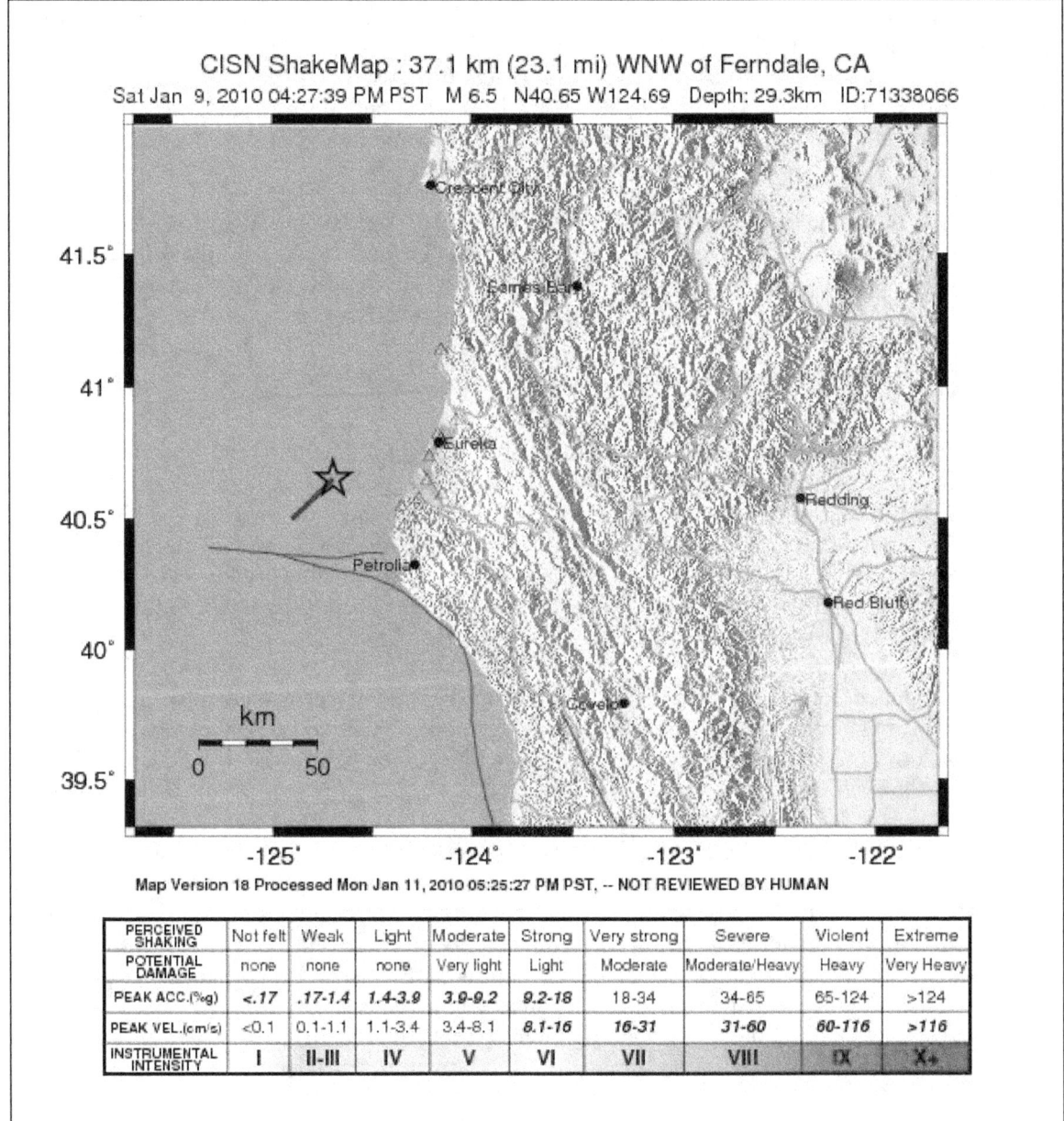

Source: USGS, http://earthquake.usgs.gov/eqcenter/shakemap/nc/shake/71338066/.

Note: Earthquake occurred 23.1 miles west-northwest of Ferndale, CA, at 4:27 p.m. on January 9, 2010, with a magnitude of 6.5. The star indicates the epicenter of the earthquake. Viewed on January 12, 2010.

Prompt Assessment of Global Earthquakes for Response (PAGER)

Another USGS product that is designed to provide nearly real-time earthquake information to emergency responders, government agencies, and the media is the Prompt Assessment of Global Earthquakes for Response, or PAGER, system.[60] This automated system rapidly assesses the number of people, cities, and regions exposed to severe shaking by an earthquake, and generally makes results available within 30 minutes. Following the determination of earthquake location and magnitude, the PAGER system calculates the degree of ground shaking using the methodology developed for ShakeMap, estimates the number of people exposed to various levels of shaking, and produces a description of the vulnerability of the exposed population and infrastructure. The vulnerability includes potential for earthquake-triggered landslides, which could be devastating, as was the case for the huge May 12, 2008, earthquake in Sichuan, China. The automated and rapid reports produced by the PAGER system provide an advantage compared to the traditional accounts from eye-witnesses on the ground or media reports, because communications networks may have been disabled from the earthquake. Emergency responders, relief organizations, and government agencies could make plans based on PAGER system reports even before getting "ground-truth" information from eye-witnesses and the media.[61] **Figure 6** shows an example of PAGER output for the January 12, 2010, magnitude 7.0 earthquake in Haiti.

Pre-disaster Planning: HAZUS-MH

FEMA developed a methodology and software program called the Hazards U.S. Multi-Hazard (HAZUS-MH).[62] The program allows a user to estimate losses from damaging earthquakes, hurricane winds, and floods before a disaster occurs. The pre-disaster estimates could provide a basis for developing mitigation plans and policies, preparing for emergencies, and planning response and recovery. HAZUS-MH combines existing scientific knowledge about earthquakes (for example, ShakeMaps, described above), engineering information that includes data on how structures respond to shaking, and geographic information system (GIS) software to produce maps and display hazards data including economic loss estimates. The loss estimates produced by HAZUS-MH include

- physical damage to residential and commercial buildings, schools, critical facilities, and infrastructure;
- economic loss, including lost jobs, business interruptions, repair and reconstruction costs; and
- social impacts, including estimates of shelter requirements, displaced households, and number of people exposed to the disaster.

In addition to furnishing information as part of earthquake mitigation efforts, HAZUS-MH can also be used to support real-time emergency response activities by state and federal agencies after a disaster. Twenty-seven HAZUS-MH user groups—cooperative ventures among private, public, and academic organizations that use the HAZUS-MH software—have formed across the United States to help foster better-informed risk management for earthquakes and other natural hazards.[63]

---

[60] See the USGS Earthquakes Hazards Program for more information, at http://earthquake.usgs.gov/earthquakes/pager/.

[61] See also USGS Fact Sheet 2007-3101 at http://pubs.usgs.gov/fs/2007/3101/.

[62] See http://www.fema.gov/plan/prevent/hazus/hz_overview.shtm.

[63] See http://www.hazus.org/.

Figure 6. Example of PAGER Output for the January 12, 2010, Magnitude 7.0 Haiti Earthquake

USGS
science for a changing world

M 7.0, HAITI REGION
Origin Time: Tue 2010-01-12 21:53:10 UTC
Location: 18.46°N 72.53°W Depth: 13 km

PAGER
Version 7
Created: 1 day, 4 hours after earthquake

Estimated Population Exposed to Earthquake Shaking

ESTIMATED POPULATION EXPOSURE (k = x1000)	- -*	- -*	5,887k*	7,261k	1,049k	571k	314k	2,246k	332k
ESTIMATED MODIFIED MERCALLI INTENSITY	I	II-III	IV	V	VI	VII	VIII	IX	X+
PERCEIVED SHAKING	Not felt	Weak	Light	Moderate	Strong	Very Strong	Severe	Violent	Extreme
POTENTIAL DAMAGE — Resistant Structures	none	none	none	V. Light	Light	Moderate	Moderate/Heavy	Heavy	V. Heavy
POTENTIAL DAMAGE — Vulnerable Structures	none	none	none	Light	Moderate	Moderate/Heavy	Heavy	V. Heavy	V. Heavy

*Estimated exposure only includes population within the map area.

Population Exposure   population per ~1 sq. km from Landscan

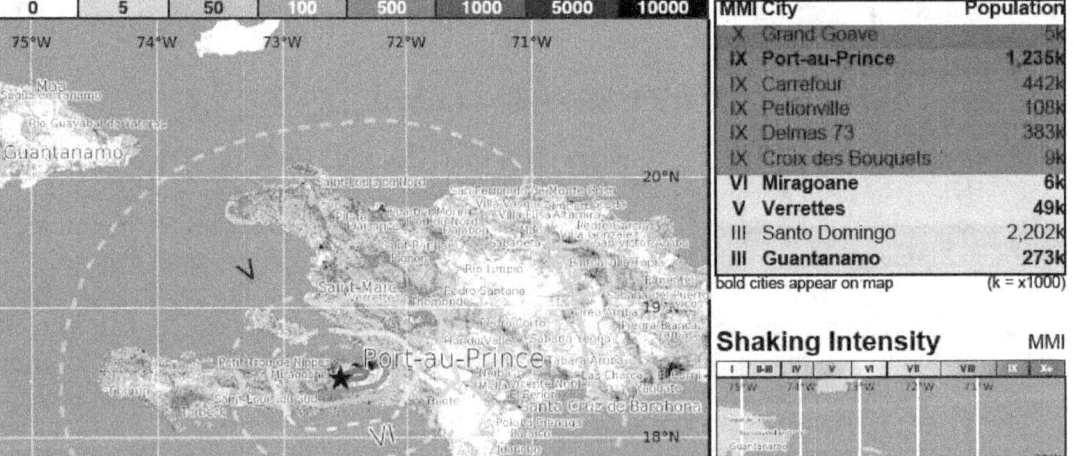

Selected City Exposure

MMI	City	Population
X	Grand Goave	5k
IX	Port-au-Prince	1,235k
IX	Carrefour	442k
IX	Petionville	108k
IX	Delmas 73	383k
IX	Croix des Bouquets	9k
VI	Miragoane	6k
V	Verrettes	49k
III	Santo Domingo	2,202k
III	Guantanamo	273k

bold cities appear on map   (k = x1000)

Shaking Intensity   MMI

Overall, the population in this region resides in structures that are vulnerable to earthquake shaking, though some resistant structures exist. On June 24, 1984 (UTC), a magnitude 6.7 earthquake 329 km East of this one struck the Dominican Republic, with estimated population exposures of 320,000 at intensity VII and 2,964,000 at intensity VI, resulting in an estimated 5 fatalities. Recent earthquakes in this area have caused landslides that may have contributed to losses.

This information was automatically generated and has not been reviewed by a seismologist.

http://earthquake.usgs.gov/pager   Event ID: us2010rja6

Source: USGS, http://earthquake.usgs.gov/earthquakes/pager/events/us/2010rja6/onepager.pdf.

Note: This is version 7 of the PAGER output, accessed on January 14, 2010.

Research — Understanding Earthquakes

U.S. Geological Survey

Under NEHRP, the USGS has responsibility for conducting targeted research into improving the basic scientific understanding of earthquake processes. The current earthquake research program at the USGS covers six broad categories:[64]

- *Borehole geophysics and rock mechanics*: studies to understand heat flow, stress, fluid pressure, and the mechanical behavior of fault-zone materials at seismogenic[65] depths to yield improved models of the earthquake cycle;

- *Crustal deformation*: studies of the distortion or deformation of the earth's surface near active faults as a result of the motion of tectonic plates;

- *Earthquake geology and paleoseismology*: studies of the history, effects, and mechanics of earthquakes;

- *Earthquake hazards*: studies of where, why, when, and how earthquakes occur;

- *Regional and whole-earth structure*: studies using seismic waves from earthquakes and man-made sources to determine the structure of the planet ranging from the local scale, to the whole crust, mantle, and even the earth's core; and

- *Strong-motion seismology, site response, and ground motion*: studies of large-amplitude ground motions and the response of engineered structures to those motions using accelerometers.

National Science Foundation

NSF supports fundamental research into understanding the earth's dynamic crust. Through its Earth Sciences Division (part of the Geosciences Directorate), NSF distributes research grants and coordinates programs investigating the crustal processes that lead to earthquakes around the globe.[66]

EarthScope

In 2003, NSF initiated a Major Research Equipment and Facilities Construction (MREFC) project called EarthScope that deploys instruments across the United States to study the structure and evolution of the North American Continent, and to investigate the physical processes that cause earthquakes and volcanic eruptions.[67] EarthScope is a multi-year project begun in 2003 that is funded by NSF and conducted in partnership with the USGS and NASA.

---

[64] See http://earthquake.usgs.gov/research/.

[65] Seismogenic means capable of generating earthquakes.

[66] See http://www.nsf.gov/div/index.jsp?div=EAR.

[67] See http://www.earthscope.org/.

EarthScope instruments are intended to form a framework for broad, integrated studies of the four-dimensional (three spatial dimensions, plus time) structure of North America. The project is divided into three main programs:

- *The San Andreas Fault Observatory at Depth (SAFOD)*, a deep borehole observatory drilled through the San Andreas fault zone close to the hypocenter of the 1966 Parkfield, CA, magnitude 6 earthquake;

- *The Plate Boundary Observatory (PBO)*, a system of GPS arrays and strainmeters[68] that measure the active boundary zone between the Pacific and North American tectonic plates in the western United States; and

- *USArray*, 400 transportable seismometers that will be deployed systematically across the United States on a uniform grid to provide a complete image of North America from continuous seismic measurements.

SAFOD and PBO are in place and providing data to the seismological community. USArray is progressing across North America and is also furnishing real-time data to seismologists. The portable array currently covers the midsection of the United States and is moving east. The installation plan calls for completing the portable array by 2013.[69]

Network for Earthquake Engineering Simulation

Through its Engineering Directorate, NSF funds the George E. Brown Jr. Network for Earthquake Engineering Simulation (NEES), a project intended to operate until 2014, aimed at understanding the effects of earthquakes on structures and materials.[70] To achieve the program's goal, the NEES facilities conduct experiments and computer simulations of how buildings, bridges, utilities, coastal regions, and materials behave during an earthquake. In the first six years of operations since 2004, 160 multiyear projects have been completed or are in progress under NEES.[71]

Conclusion

At present earthquakes can be neither accurately predicted nor prevented, and in its 1990 reauthorization NEHRP shifted its program emphasis from prediction to hazard reduction. The program's focus has been on understanding the earthquake hazard and its risk to populations and infrastructure in the United States, developing effective measures to reduce earthquake hazards, and promoting the adoption of earthquake hazards reduction measures in vulnerable areas.

---

[68] A strainmeter is a tool used by seismologists to measure the motion of one point relative to another.

[69] See http://www.usarray.org/maps.

[70] Management for NEES has been headquartered at Purdue University's Discovery Park since October 1, 2009. Institutions participating in NEES include Cornell University; Lehigh University; Oregon State University; Rensselaer Polytechnical Institute; University of Buffalo-State University of New York; University of California-Berkeley; University of California-Davis; University of California-Los Angeles; University of California-San Diego; University of California-Santa Barbara; University of Colorado-Boulder; University of Illinois at Urbana-Champaign; University of Minnesota; University of Nevada-Reno; and University of Texas at Austin. See http://www.nees.org/.

[71] See http://nees.org/about.

Legislation to modify NEHRP in the 108th Congress (P.L. 108-360) reflected congressional concerns about how well the four NEHRP agencies coordinated their efforts to maximize the program's potential. If legislation is introduced in the 112th Congress to modify the program and reauthorize appropriations, Congress may consider evaluating how effectively the agencies have responded to Congress's direction in P.L. 108-360 to improve coordination since 2004.

In the 111th Congress, legislation introduced to make changes to NEHRP, H.R. 3820, reemphasized that approach but cast it in terms of hazard *mitigation* by stating that a major goal for the program should be "to reduce the loss of life and damage to communities and infrastructure through increasing the adoption of hazard mitigation measures." The bill further emphasized the social aspects of mitigating earthquake hazards, calling for research to better understand institutional, social, behavioral, and economic factors that influence how risk mitigation is implemented, in addition to the traditional research into understanding how, why, and where earthquakes occur.

The emphasis on mitigation proposed by H.R. 3820 in the 111th Congress reflects at least two fundamental challenges to increasing the nation's resiliency to earthquakes, and to most other major natural hazards such as hurricanes and major floods. The first is to assess whether social, behavioral, and economic factors can be understood in sufficient degree to devise strategies that influence behavior to mitigate risk posed by the hazard. Put simply, what motivates people and communities to adopt risk mitigation measures that address the potential hazard? A second challenge, which is more squarely an issue for Congress, is how to measure the effectiveness of NEHRP more quantitatively. It is inherently difficult to capture precisely, in terms of dollars saved or fatalities prevented, the effectiveness of mitigation measures taken before an earthquake occurs. A major earthquake in a populated urban area within the United States would cause damage, and a question becomes how much damage would be prevented by mitigation strategies underpinned by the NEHRP program.

A precise relationship between earthquake mitigation measures, NEHRP and other federal earthquake-related activities, and reduced losses from an actual earthquake may never be possible. However, as more accurate seismic hazard maps evolve, as understanding of the relationship between ground motion and building safety improves, and as new tools for issuing warnings and alerts such as ShakeMap and PAGER are devised, trends denoting the effectiveness of mitigation strategies and NEHRP activities may emerge more clearly. Without an ability to precisely predict earthquakes, Congress is likely to face an ongoing challenge in determining the most effective federal approach to increasing the nation's resilience to low-probability but high-impact natural hazards, such as major earthquakes.

Author Contact Information

Peter Folger
Specialist in Energy and Natural Resources Policy
pfolger@crs.loc.gov, 7-1517